DISCARD

BILL GATES

By Lauren Lee

WORLD ALMANAC® LIBRARY

Please visit our web site at: www.worldalmanaclibrary.com
For a free color catalog describing World Almanac® Library's list
of high-quality books and multimedia programs, call 1-800-848-2928 (USA)
or 1-800-387-3178 (Canada). World Almanac® Library's fax: (414) 332-3567.

Library of Congress Cataloging-in-Publication Data

Lee, Lauren, 1963-
    Bill Gates / by Lauren Lee.
        p. cm. — (Trailblazers of the modern world)
    Includes bibliographical references and index.
    Summary: A biography of the man whose vision of the computer industry changed the way people
live and work, and who now plans to improve the world with the billions he has earned from Microsoft.
    ISBN 0-8368-5077-7 (lib. bdg.)
    ISBN 0-8368-5237-0 (softcover)
    1. Gates, Bill, 1955—Juvenile literature. 2. Microsoft Corporation—History—Juvenile literature.
3. Businessmen—United States—Biography—Juvenile literature. 4. Computer software industry—
United States—History—Juvenile literature. [1. Gates, Bill, 1955-. 2. Microsoft Corporation—History.
3. Businesspeople. 4. Computer software industry.] I. Title. II. Series.
HD9696.63.U62G374495   2002
338.7'610053'092—dc21
[B]   2002072225

This edition first published in 2002 by
World Almanac® Library
330 West Olive Street, Suite 100
Milwaukee, WI 53212 USA

This edition © 2002 by World Almanac® Library.

Project editor: Mark J. Sachner
Design and page production: Scott M. Krall
Photo research: Diane Laska-Swanke
Editor: Betsy Rasmussen
Indexer: Walter Kronenberg
Production direction: Susan Ashley

Photo credits: © AP/Wide World Photos: 9, 20, 23, 30, 31, 34 bottom, 36 bottom, 38, 42; © Bettmann/CORBIS: 7, 10, 12
bottom, 16 both, 17 bottom, 21; © Bob Rowan; Progressive Image/CORBIS: 15; © Bolante/Reuters/Getty Images: 24, 37,
41; © Burroughs/Getty Images: 5; © Callister/Getty Images: 40; © Christensen/Getty Images: 43; Computer Museum
of America: 25; Courtesy of Lakeside School: 18; © Crosby/Getty Images: 36 top; © Deborah Feingold/Getty Images: 34
top; Diane Laska-Swanke: 32; © Doug Wilson/CORBIS: 28 bottom; © Ed Kashi/CORBIS: 4; © Getty Images: 28 top;
© Gibbons/Reuters/Getty Images: 29; © Hulton Archive/Getty Images: 11 bottom, 12 top, 13 both, 22, 39 bottom;
© Hulton-Deutsch Collection/CORBIS: 17 top; © Lynn Goldsmith/CORBIS: cover; NASA courtesy of Getty Images:
11 top; © Reuters/Getty Images: 39 top; © Sugita/Reuters/Getty Images: 6 bottom; © Walker/Getty Images: 33;
© Wurzer/Getty Images: 6 top

Printed in the United States of America

1 2 3 4 5 6 7 8 9 06 05 04 03 02

TABLE of CONTENTS

Words that appear in the glossary are printed in **boldface**
type the first time they occur in the text.

CHAPTER 1

VISIONARY

When this photo of Bill Gates was taken in 1987, he was already one of the leaders of the U.S. computer industry.

In his rumpled khakis and bad haircut, Bill Gates rocks back and forth. He interrupts one of his engineers, saying, "That's the stupidest thing I've ever heard." He has not been home to sleep. His shirt is stained, and pizza crusts litter the desk.

Judging by his appearance, you would hardly guess that he is the richest man in the United States. Even though he is in his late forties, he still looks boyish, bookish, and shy. As head of Microsoft, however, he makes the software that powers most of the world's personal computers. By 2001, Microsoft employed more than forty thousand people in five dozen countries.

Whichever personal computer you use—Dell, Compaq, IBM, Gateway, Hewlett-Packard, or some other brand—you almost certainly use Microsoft Windows as your **operating system**. If you have an Apple Macintosh computer, you may use a Microsoft program like Word or Internet Explorer. And if you are into video games, chances are good that you own, or have tried, the Microsoft Xbox game system. This did not happen by accident. Gates is a visionary—a person with a clear idea of what the future will look like and the ability to make it happen.

A Computer in Every Home

When Gates and his friend and business partner Paul Allen founded Microsoft in New Mexico in 1975, Gates was thinking big. He and Allen were writing software for the computer revolution, and they wanted everyone to buy it. His thinking was revolutionary, because most people had never thought of having their own personal computer. Gates predicted that there would be "a computer in every home and Microsoft software on every computer."

Gates has fought his way to the top. He takes his vision and himself very seriously. He is willing to go to any length to achieve his goal. If he works hard, so do his employees. If he wants a contract, he will get a contract. He can be insensitive and mean. He does not much care if people like him. He has made powerful enemies.

At the same time, his new vision is to use billions of the dollars he has earned through Microsoft to make the world a healthier and happier place, especially for children. He and his wife Melinda have given enormous sums of money to help prevent childhood diseases. They also are working to improve

Gates likes to think big, whether he is promoting a new computer operating system or giving billions of dollars to charity.

health care services throughout the world and to make sure that schools and libraries everywhere have computers and Internet access. This new vision may be every bit as revolutionary as his original vision of the personal computer.

Microsoft, the world's largest and most powerful software company, is the centerpiece of Gates's financial empire.

A video game player gives Microsoft's Xbox a whirl in Tokyo, Japan.

How Much Money Does Bill Gates Have?

Each year, *Forbes* magazine ranks the richest people in the world. Since 1998, Bill Gates has been ranked number one.

Much of his wealth is based on the value of Microsoft stock. During the late 1990s, as the U.S. economy boomed, the value of Gates's holdings rose higher and higher. At the end of the decade, however, Microsoft's stock price dropped, and so did Gates's wealth. Even so, he still has a personal fortune greater than the annual product of many countries.

Year	Worth
1998	$51,000,000,000 ($51.0 billion)
1999	$90,000,000,000 ($90.0 billion)
2000	$60,000,000,000 ($60.0 billion)
2001	$58,700,000,000 ($58.7 billion)
2002	$52,800,000,000 ($52.8 billion)

Source: *Forbes*

FAMILY TIES

William Henry Gates III was born on October 28, 1955, in Seattle, Washington. He has deep roots in the Evergreen State. Counting the two children of Bill and Melinda Gates, Jennifer and Rory, the Gates family has lived in Washington for five generations.

On both his father's and his mother's sides, Bill's family has given him a pioneering spirit, independence, competitiveness, and a commitment to making the world a better place.

THE GATES TRADITION

One of Bill's great-grandfathers, William Henry Gates Sr., was a pioneer who left Pennsylvania for the Northwest in the 1880s. A brave and independent man, he made his living by making wagon deliveries in the Seattle area until he moved his family to Nome, Alaska, where gold was discovered in the 1890s. The miners chased gold northward, but Bill's great-grandfather struck it rich by starting a business instead.

Some of these miners had come to Alaska with little more than the clothes on their backs, so they needed

A great-grandfather of Bill Gates made his fortune selling supplies to miners like these who came to Alaska during the Gold Rush of the 1890s.

supplies for their new homes. The elder Gates found a way to help. He sold furniture to transplanted miners. His son also started his own business. By the age of eight, Bill Gates's grandfather was selling newspapers to the miners so they could read the news from the towns they had left behind.

In the 1910s, after moving back to Washington state, great-grandfather Gates started a hotel and another furniture business. When the business became successful, Gates's grandfather became the furniture store's manager. His son Billy—Bill Gates's father—was born in 1925. Billy was originally called William Henry Gates III (the same name his world-famous son uses), but before he went into the army, he changed his name to the less imposing William H. Gates Jr.

Bill Gates's father was also a businessman from an early age. He and a friend published a newspaper. At age thirteen, they made money by selling advertising space. As an adult, Bill Gates's father became a successful lawyer, marrying Bill's mother, Mary Maxwell, in 1951. Bill Gates was the second of their three children and their only son.

Gates Family Facts

Bill Gates:	Born in 1955.
Sisters:	Kristi, born in 1954; Libby, born in 1964. Libby has two children.
Wife:	Married Melinda French in 1994, now the cochair of the Gates Foundation.
Children:	Jennifer Katharine, born in 1996; Rory John, born in 1999.
Father:	William H. Gates Jr. is the cochair of the Gates Foundation.
Mother:	Mary Maxwell Gates died in 1994.

THE MAXWELLS

A pioneering and independent spirit came to Bill from his mother's family as well. From the Maxwells, Bill learned to give generously to others. This trait is defining the second half of Bill's life.

Mary Maxwell's grandfather, James Willard Maxwell, was born in Iowa. After his family moved to Lincoln, Nebraska, he started his career in banking at the bottom (literally!) by digging a cellar for a local bank president. Maxwell worked his way up as an errand boy and then a cashier. In 1892, he moved with his wife to the town of South Bend, Washington. He made powerful friends who helped him become successful in politics and finance.

He was elected to the local school board and to the offices of mayor and state legislator. Maxwell was very competitive, and he also had a strong work ethic—a belief in working as hard as possible to achieve any goal. He also believed in giving back to the town where he had made his money and raised his family. Each year, he donated enough turkeys to feed a thousand people who did not have enough money to buy their own Thanksgiving dinner. He believed that rich people had a duty to share some of their wealth with people who were less fortunate.

Like her grandfather, Mary Maxwell Gates had a strong commitment to helping others. By the time Bill and his sisters were in school, Mary spent much of her time doing charitable work.

When Bill and his sisters came home from school, they were greeted by Mary's mother, Adelle Maxwell. Grandmother (or "Gam") Adelle was a spirited and competitive woman. She played games with the Gates children and taught them how to play cards, especially bridge, one of her favorite games. She gave Bill his boyhood nickname Trey (for "the third"), which is a term for the three in a deck of cards.

While Bill Gates was growing up, the United States was facing many challenges. One of these challenges was the **cold war**. The cold war was the rivalry between two superpowers, the United States and the **Soviet Union** (a former country that included Russia).

This superpower rivalry affected many areas of American life. To compete with the Soviet Union, the United States government spent large sums of money on new weapons. The government also spent money on science and math education to train future scientists. Billions of dollars were used for the space program, the defense industries, and computers and computer networking development. The decision to invest in those areas still affects the way we live today.

SEATTLE WORLD'S FAIR

Seattle held a World's Fair in 1962, when Bill was not quite seven years old. It was a "huge event, a neat deal,"

Superpower rivalry led to the "space race" between the United States and the Soviet Union during the cold war era.

At the Seattle World's Fair in 1962, the General Electric Pavilion (left foreground) made a major impression on the young Bill Gates.

Both the IBM Pavilion and the Space Needle behind it pointed the way to the future at the 1962 World's Fair.

he later said, and the Gates family went to every pavilion. The fair, which had the theme "Century 21," was meant to be fun, but it also had a serious purpose. It was meant to show how technology—the practical use of science—could help the United States win the cold war.

At this World's Fair, Seattle's new Space Needle pointed the way upward toward the future. One exhibit showed the *Freedom 7* space capsule, a milestone in the U.S. effort to put astronauts in space.

The young Bill was particularly excited by the computer exhibits. The **mainframe** computers of International Business Machines (IBM) could translate words and calculate satellite flight paths. The American Library Association's Univac computer stored and retrieved information from books. These computers were as big as a room and very slow, capable of not much more computing power than today's simple calculator.

The General Electric Pavilion made a bigger impression. A "GE Living" display showed what were radical inventions in 1962. The display included a large-screen color television (most televisions then were small and black and white) and an all-electronic home library. The General Electric Pavilion even had an early version of a "home computer" that could keep records, write checks, and help with shopping.

Designed and built in the 1950s, these Univac mainframe computers (left and facing page, bottom) dwarfed the people who ran them. Inside each computer was a maze of wires, tubes, and other complicated components (above).

PUBLIC SCHOOL DAYS

Although Bill was supersmart and his family was well-off, his school years were far from easy. First, unlike most students, he was left-handed. This made him feel different. Second, he moved constantly. He got into trouble for pacing, rocking, and tapping all the time. Third, he was the youngest in his class and felt clumsy, shy, and unpopular.

At the same time, his mental feats were legendary. He learned multiplication within hours. He wrote a fourteen-page paper on the human body in one hour. He had read the entire *World Book Encyclopedia* from cover to cover by the time he was nine years old. He also read a lot of adult science fiction, including books by Isaac Asimov and Arthur C. Clarke, popular sci-fi writers.

"I'm Thinking"

Bill Gates could be a difficult child, both in school and at home. Bill was impatient and rude, even with his own parents when they did not think the same way he did. Once, when he was late to join his family for an outing, he told his mother that he was too busy to leave.

"What are you doing?" she demanded.

"I'm thinking," he answered.

"You're thinking?" she asked.

"Yes, Mother, I'm thinking," he replied angrily. "Have you ever tried thinking?"

To his father, he said while in sixth grade, "Don't you ever think?"

ENROLLMENT AT LAKESIDE

In 1967, after Bill completed the sixth grade in public school, his parents decided to enroll him in a private academy. They chose the exclusive, boys-only Lakeside School. Bill soon developed a reputation as Lakeside's smartest student. He was also the smallest student in his class (and awkward, with size-thirteen feet). He did not hesitate to put other students down, and he laughed at people who were slower than he to answer questions.

Gates got more freedom and individual attention at Lakeside School because there were fewer students there than in public school. During this time, Bill became interested in Napoleon Bonaparte, who ruled France as an emperor in the early 1800s. Bill read all he could about this small man who conquered much of Europe.

Bill's grades at Lakeside averaged B, with As in math balancing the lower grades he received in subjects that did not interest him. He was fascinated by math and was gifted in the subject. One teacher noticed how Bill would find clever shortcuts to solve problems.

Even though he made some enemies at school, he also made some close friends. One of them was Paul Allen, with whom he later started Microsoft. Another was Kent Evans, who, although he died while still a Lakeside student, was one of the most important influences on Bill's life. What bound these three boys together was a machine that arrived at Lakeside in 1968—the school's first computer.

One of today's handheld calculators looks tiny when compared with a 1950s mainframe, but it has almost as much computing power.

CHAPTER 4

THE LAKESIDE PROGRAMMERS GROUP

The earliest "computers" were mechanical devices such as this abacus.

This 1909 photo shows a Victor adding machine, another important step in the development of the modern computer.

A year after Bill Gates enrolled at Lakeside, the school got its first computer. Actually, it did not look much like a computer by current standards. It would seem primitive today, like a cave compared to a house. But it was enough to send Bill on his life's path.

The new machine was an ASR-33 Teletype, consisting of a keyboard, a device that read what was typed, and a printer. The teletype was connected through a telephone handset to a Programmable Data Computer (PDP-10), manufactured by the Digital Equipment Corporation (DEC). The PDP-10 was called a time-sharing computer because it was shared by several different schools and companies.

Like the other computer users, Lakeside had to pay for the computer time its students used. The fees soon became very expensive because the boys were using the ASR-33 so much. To finance their children's efforts, the Lakeside Mothers Club—which included Bill's mother, Mary—held a rummage sale to raise money to buy more computer time. They raised $3,000, which they had hoped would last a year. Bill and his friends had become so obsessed with using the computer that they used up the whole year's budget in a few weeks. The boys were so fascinated that they skipped gym class to work in the computer lab.

Lakeside's math teacher taught Bill how to use the computer. Within a week, Bill and his friends knew more about **programming** than the teacher. All programs had to be written in **BASIC** (short for "Beginners' All-

purpose Symbolic Instruction Code"), which is a simple language for telling a computer what to do. Bill wrote programs to solve math problems and play tic-tac-toe.

COMPUTER BUDDIES

Bill's computer buddies included two especially close friends. The first, Kent Evans, was a minister's son. Like Bill, Kent was talented in math, and he influenced Bill to think of computers as a pathway to business success. As junior high students, they read *Fortune*, a magazine written for adult business leaders. The computer-obsessed Kent was late with his work in every subject all the time because he would not leave the computer lab!

Another important friend of Bill's was Paul Allen, and they remain close today. Allen, who is now one of the world's richest men, was two years older than Gates. He was crazy about reading; his parents were both librarians. Paul was a devoted fan of *Popular Electronics* magazine. He was also very fond of science fiction. It was a good way to imagine how the future might be shaped by technology. Paul had a special interest in hardware, the

physical machinery of computing, while Bill was fascinated by software, the programs that made the machinery work.

A Tragic Accident

In 1972, Gates's close friend Kent Evans died in a mountaineering accident. He lost his footing and fell at least 600 feet (183 meters) down a snowy slope and glacier.

Gates still credits Evans with helping him develop his business instincts. Decades later, Bill said, "I can still remember Kent's telephone number."

WRITING PROGRAMS FOR FUN AND PROFIT

With Gates watching, Paul Allen works the teletype at Lakeside School.

Together, Bill and his friends formed the Lakeside Programmers Group (LPG). "I was the mover," Gates recalled. "I was the guy who said, 'Let's call the real world and try to sell something to it.'"

Although they were still only schoolboys, they managed to persuade a computer firm, Information Sciences Inc. (ISI), to allow them to write a program that would handle the company's payroll. In exchange for their services, ISI would provide them with free access time on the firm's PDP-10 computer.

The program was to be written in COBOL (short for "Common Business Oriented Language"), a computer language new to the students. The job turned out to be much more difficult than the young men had expected, and they quarreled over how the work should be divided. When Allen tried to take over the project, he and Gates almost split up, but Paul soon realized that he could not do the coding by himself. He needed Bill's help. Would Bill agree to stay on? "OK," said Gates, "but I'm in charge, and I'll get used to being in charge, and it'll be hard to deal with me from now on unless I'm in charge."

Under Bill's leadership, the LPG members said that they would be done with the payroll program sooner than they could actually finish it. They delivered the program in time, but it was full of **bugs**. The LPG then had to hustle to fix the program. This pattern—promising an unrealistic deadline and then scrambling to fix the mistakes—is often mentioned by people who dislike Gates. Critics of Microsoft complain that Gates's company still follows the same practice today.

NEW PROJECTS

In 1970, Lakeside merged with a girls-only school, St. Nicholas. Lakeside hired Gates and Evans to computerize the schedule. While working on this very complex problem, the programmers slept in the teachers' lounge at school. Bill got so involved in his work that he did not comb his hair or bathe. His bedroom floor was littered with dirty laundry and computer paper. By the time the job was done, Bill had been paid at least $4,000 for his programming work—a lot of money for a sixteen-year-old in the early 1970s.

While still at Lakeside, Gates and Allen formed a company called Traf-O-Data. The company tried to

Gates told the story of his Lakeside days and discussed the future of computing in his book *The Road Ahead*, originally published in 1995.

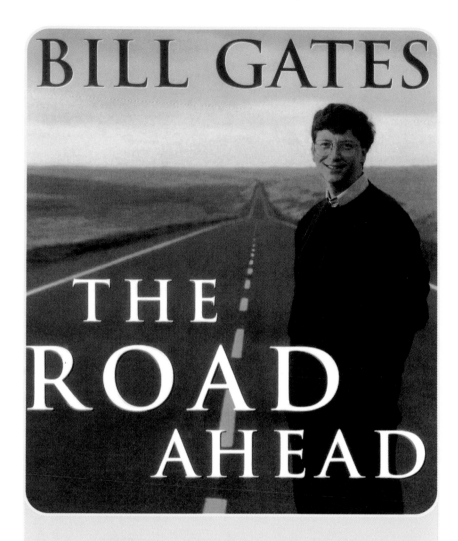

Making His Own Schedule

Being the programming genius behind Lakeside's class schedule had some fringe benefits. Here is a story Gates told in his book *The Road Ahead* (1995):

One of the programs I wrote was the one that scheduled students in classes. I **surreptitiously** *added a few instructions and found myself nearly the only guy in a class full of girls. As I said before, it was hard to tear myself away from a machine at which I could so unambiguously demonstrate success. I was hooked.*

gather and sell information about traffic patterns to city governments so that planners could time traffic lights and schedule repair work in ways that prevented traffic jams. The boys developed a primitive computer system using a simple code represented by holes punched in a roll of computer tape. For the first time, Bill invested money in a business in order to build a computer. Bill and Paul even hired an engineer, and they continued to work on the project for years. Although Traf-O-Data was never a great success, it did help Bill learn how to build a business.

How to keep rush-hour traffic moving was a major problem for city governments in the 1970s, just as it is today. Gates and Allen formed Traf-O-Data to help highway planners prevent traffic jams.

Life at Lakeside was not all computers. Gates acted in school plays, was named a National Merit Scholar, and was accepted to Princeton, Yale, and Harvard. On his SATs, he scored a perfect 800 in math and in the low 700s for verbal. In 1973, he headed east to Harvard with the idea of becoming a lawyer like his father. But thoughts of software and business were never far from his mind.

CHAPTER 5

FROM HARVARD TO MICROSOFT

The summer before he enrolled at Harvard, Gates and Allen each got jobs as programmers at a salary of $165 per week. They worked for TRW, a government defense contractor. They helped design software to measure and control the flow of electricity from hydroelectric plants on the Columbia River.

Gates entered Harvard in 1973. Eventually, he would become one of the university's most famous dropouts.

The young men continued the intense, obsessive work style they had developed while at Lakeside. Gates, Allen, and another friend shared a small apartment. They worked through the night, skipped baths, and lived on pizza and Tang, a powdered orange drink. When the student programmers needed a break, they would work on Traf-O-Data or play games. Some of their favorite games were Go, an Asian strategy game, and chess. Intensely competitive even at play, Bill would sometimes flip over the chessboard if he was losing. Gates still hates to lose—as Microsoft's rivals have learned over the last two decades.

COLLEGE FRESHMAN

In the autumn of 1973, Gates entered Harvard University, one of the nation's most competitive schools.

Even at Harvard, Bill was smart enough to get special attention. Harvard named him a "National Scholar" and enrolled him in a special math class. Here, Bill finally met people who were even smarter than he was.

Bill's record at Harvard was spotty. He did not want people to think he had to work hard for grades. He ignored some of his "easy" courses, rarely showing up for class, and then he worked feverishly at the end of the term. An eager reader, Bill relied on a near photographic memory. He could take a mental "picture" of a page of writing and remember what was on it. He used this technique to cram for exams in courses he had ignored earlier in the semester.

Gates cared more about his computer work than about his appearance or health. Although his family had money, he wore ratty clothes. He spoke lines of computer

Steve Ballmer, the Chief Executive Officer of Microsoft, became friends with Gates while the two men were living in the same Harvard dormitory.

Programmer Culture

Computer programmers and **hackers** live in their own world. They become so immersed in working on their computers that nothing else seems to matter. Their minds are on the screen, and their hearts are in solving problems. Here is how Steve Ballmer, a friend of Gates's who became a top Microsoft executive, described what Bill was like during their college days:

I heard about this crazy guy. He never put sheets on his bed. He went home for Christmas vacation with the door to his room open, the lights on, money on the desk, the windows open, and it was raining, and Bill was in Seattle.

Paul Allen

Paul Gardner Allen, childhood friend of Bill Gates and cofounder of Microsoft, was born in Seattle, Washington, on January 21, 1953. After graduating from the Lakeside School in 1971, he enrolled in Washington State University; like Gates, however, he never completed his studies.

Allen left Microsoft after learning in 1982 that he had Hodgkin's disease, a form of cancer. Since then, through his Microsoft stock and other businesses, he has become one of the world's wealthiest people. *Forbes* magazine estimated his holdings at more than $25 billion in 2002. He owns the Portland Trail Blazers basketball team and the Seattle Seahawks football team. He has also given generously to many worthy causes, especially in the Northwest. A music lover who plays electric guitar, he developed the Experience Music Project in Seattle, the home city of one of his heroes, guitarist Jimi Hendrix.

Paul Allen gave new meaning to the term "smash hit" at opening ceremonies in June 2000 for Seattle's Experience Music Project—he picked up a glass guitar and sent it crashing to the ground.

code in his sleep. He and his friends played poker and lived on hamburgers and pizza. He pushed himself to exhaustion. At the end of his first year, he became sick enough to spend a week in the hospital.

Bill put his interests above getting along with people, too. As a freshman, he talked his way into the higher-level computer classes, which were usually limited to older students. He would sit in class and wait for other students to make a mistake; then he would tell them that they were wrong. "Gates had a bad personality and a great intellect," said one professor. "In a place like Harvard, where there are a lot of bright kids, . . . some tend to be nice and others obnoxious. He was the latter."

Gates's Harvard career skidded to a halt after Paul Allen showed him a story he had spotted on the cover of a *Popular Electronics* magazine in December 1974. Allen, bored with college, had gotten a job with a Boston technology company and was again spending a lot of time with Gates, his old Lakeside School buddy. The magazine cover pictured what it called the "World's First **Microcomputer** Kit to Rival Commercial Models." A cheap computer almost anyone could build at home—this was the development that Gates and Allen had been preparing themselves for since 1968.

The cover featured a picture of the Altair 8800 computer, made by a company called Micro Instrumentation and Telemetry Systems (MITS). Allen and Gates investigated the story and discovered that this "microcomputer" was basically a box with blinking lights—it had no keyboard, no monitor, and no operating system.

Gates and Allen knew that without software the Altair 8800 was nothing but an empty shell. They contacted MITS and told company officials they had a software program (a version of BASIC) that would make the Altair 8800 run. This was a bluff—they had not written the program yet.

Fortunately for Gates and Allen, MITS also was bluffing, because the Altair 8800 was not yet ready to be shipped to consumers. The head of MITS said

The original Altair 8800 was almost useless until Gates and Allen wrote an operating system for it.

he needed a month before he could meet with Paul. Allen pretended to be disappointed, but really he and Gates were glad, because they needed the time to adapt the old code they had used for Traf-O-Data.

Gates took a lot of risks to meet the MITS deadline. He worked at an intense pace around the clock, skipping meals, skipping classes, and using the Harvard computer lab without permission. "Paul and I didn't sleep much and lost track of night and day," Gates later wrote. "When I did fall asleep, it was often at my desk or on the floor. Some days I didn't eat or see anyone. But after five weeks, our BASIC was written—and the world's first microcomputer software company was born. In time we named it 'Microsoft.'"

NEW HORIZONS IN NEW MEXICO

When Allen arrived in Albuquerque, New Mexico, where MITS was located, everyone was disappointed. Allen was surprised that the MITS "headquarters" was a small shop in a seedy part of town. Ed Roberts, the founder of MITS, was surprised that his software engineer was so young and so broke. When the software actually worked and a simple program ran without crashing, however, Roberts agreed to use their product.

MITS wanted to be the only company with the legal right to use Bill's version of BASIC. Under this arrangement, MITS would own the sole rights to distribute the program and include it with each Altair 8800 it shipped. When MITS sold an Altair with Bill's program in it, Bill made money. Bill was dependent on MITS to do his selling for him, however. He learned quickly that this was not the route to big profits, and later, he changed his strategy.

Gates and Allen knew they were onto something big, and they took big risks in order to cash in on it. Bill had gotten into trouble at Harvard for letting Allen, a nonstudent, work on the campus computers and for using the university's machines for his and Paul's personal profit. Gates was disciplined, and he lost his free computer time.

Founding Principles

In a 1997 E-mail to David Bank, a reporter for the *Wall Street Journal*, Gates explained the core ideas behind the founding of Microsoft as a software company twenty-two years earlier:

1. Software [is] the key to unlocking exponential improvement in the power of computers.

2. Software should be separate from hardware because the way you manage and attract great people is different.

3. Software should be separate from hardware because you allow consumers to choose whatever hardware they think is best.

4. Software will eventually make computers totally natural and easy to work with.

5. Selling software in volume allows for low prices even while spending increasing amounts on research and development.

I don't see any change that makes me think something is wrong with these principles.

While living in New Mexico, Gates ran afoul of the law by driving without a license.

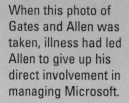

When this photo of Gates and Allen was taken, illness had led Allen to give up his direct involvement in managing Microsoft.

Allen moved from Boston to Albuquerque and began working for MITS full time. In 1975, he and Gates formed a new company, which they called "Microsoft"—a name that combined parts of the words "microcomputer" and "software." According to their agreement, Bill owned about two-thirds of the company, and Allen owned about one-third.

By 1976, Gates and Allen had grown unhappy with MITS. Customers were not getting their computers on time. The hardware was not very good. Only MITS could sell Bill's version of BASIC. But because MITS was not very successful at marketing its own products, Gates was earning little profit.

Gates dropped out of Harvard and moved to

Albuquerque during the winter of 1976–1977. He and Allen also recruited some of their computer friends to come to Albuquerque and join them. By this time, the Microsoft founders had a new business plan. Never again would they tie themselves to any single computer hardware company. Microsoft would develop operating systems for different types of computers and earn money by licensing its software to different firms.

MITS was not happy about the new plan. It wanted to keep its exclusive right to sell Microsoft's version of BASIC. MITS sued Microsoft, but Gates eventually won the court case. Once again, Gates's risk-

taking had paid off. In the meantime, he had begun selling his brand of BASIC to other computer companies, such as Commodore, Tandy (Radio Shack), and several Japanese manufacturers.

BASIC was on its way, and so was Microsoft. In 1978, Gates and Allen decided to move Microsoft's head-quarters from Albuquerque to the Seattle area. It was time to go home.

CHAPTER 6

SOFTWARE POWERHOUSE

Around 1980, the computer hardware business was starting to change. Before that time, most computer buyers were large corporations, government agencies, and schools that had enough money, technical know-how, and storage space to run their own machines. From the early 1980s onward, however, more and more individuals and small businesses wanted and could afford computers.

International Business Machines (IBM), a maker of large mainframe computers, realized that it would have to change its strategy in order to keep up with changes in the market. When IBM developed the personal computer (PC), it decided to focus on the hardware. IBM asked Microsoft to develop an operating system (OS) within a year. True to form, despite the impossibly short time frame, Microsoft agreed to do it.

Introduced in 1981, the IBM PC set a new standard for personal computing.

MS-DOS AND THE IBM PC

Microsoft employees from those days remember that period of time as if sharing memories of war. The project was utterly secret, and they worked day and night. Most of the early Microsoft programmers were young, white males, just like Gates and his friends. They were trained, available, and willing to work. Such a schedule would be hard on someone with a family, and women at that time were generally not a part of the computer culture.

Luckily, Gates knew someone with an operating system that could be adapted to the IBM PC. The man's name was Tim Paterson, and he worked for Seattle Computer Products. Gates and Allen negotiated with Seattle Computer to use the company's operating system, never revealing that they were ultimately selling it to IBM.

When Seattle Computer found out how its product was eventually used, company officials felt angry and cheated. Microsoft had squeezed them out of the deal. Tactics like these have made Microsoft very controversial in the computer industry. Many people admire Gates for his tough-minded business strategy. Others take a less positive view. A competitor of Microsoft called the firm "a great white shark that knows no boundaries. All it knows is its appetite. When it gets hungry, it eats."

At the heart of every personal computer is the microprocessor, a powerful chip no bigger than a postage stamp.

The Most Famous Thing That Bill Gates Never Said

People who do not like Bill Gates often point to a "prediction" he made that turned out to be just plain wrong. In 1981, so the story goes, Gates made this statement about how much memory (**RAM**) a personal computer would need: "640K of memory should be enough for anybody." Since today's computers usually have 200, 400, or even 800 times that much RAM, Gates's "prediction" would be far off the mark—if he had ever made the prediction. But Gates denies he ever said any such thing. In 1996 he wrote:

I've said some stupid things and some wrong things, but not that. No one involved in computers would ever say that a certain amount of memory is enough for all time.

Under the deal Gates reached with IBM, Microsoft received a fee for every PC sold by IBM that was bundled with the Microsoft disk operating system, or MS-**DOS**. Gates also had the legal right to sell his operating system to companies that competed with IBM. This kind of deal, known as a **nonexclusive licensing agreement**, was to become the basis of Microsoft's success.

The first IBM PCs came out in 1981. Almost immediately, because of IBM's tremendous power and influence, they became the standard in the personal computer industry. Other companies also made PCs, which were commonly known as PC **clones**. These machines also were bundled with Microsoft's software. Thanks to its nonexclusive licensing agreements, Microsoft made money on every IBM PC and every clone sold.

This Apple IIe computer ran a version of BASIC licensed from Microsoft.

A BITE OF THE APPLE

In the meantime, another company was developing a different kind of personal computer. While Bill Gates was pulling all-nighters in the mid-1970s to work on BASIC, Steve Jobs and his friend Steve Wozniak were building a machine in the Jobs family garage that was called the Apple. Gates was no stranger to the world of Apple. Applesoft BASIC for Apple II computers was licensed from Microsoft.

In the early 1980s, Jobs showed Gates a version of Apple's newest product—the Macintosh. The Mac's most striking aspect was its **interface**, the way the computer interacted with the user. Instead of complicated commands,

In 1984, Apple's cofounder Steve Jobs introduced the Macintosh, a computer that was much easier to use than the IBM PC.

the Mac used icons, or small pictures, and a mouse. All the user had to do was "point and click." This **graphical user interface**, or GUI, was much simpler than typing in computer commands; almost anyone could use a computer with icons and a mouse.

It seemed like a unique idea, but in fact, it had been developed at Xerox's Palo Alto Research Center (PARC) in the 1970s. The problem with a graphical user interface was that it required a lot of memory, which was much more costly at that time than it is today. Most PCs lacked the memory to make a GUI work.

WINDOWS

Apple had a business plan that was different from IBM's. For many years, Apple refused to license clones, and it kept tight control over both the Macintosh hardware and operating system. Apple did, however, contract with Microsoft to write some software for the Macintosh. One result was Microsoft Word, which is now widely used on both PCs and Macs.

By the mid-1980s, PCs were becoming cheaper because more companies made them. Apples were expensive, and their software was limited. What the Mac still had going for it was the graphical user interface. Gates decided that Microsoft would compete by developing a GUI that would run on IBM PCs and clones. This

On the floppy disk held by Gates in this 1985 photo was an early version of Microsoft Windows. The program gave the PC a friendlier interface.

Steve Jobs shocked many Macintosh users in 1997 when he revealed Microsoft's large investment in Apple.

new operating system—called Windows—was first announced in November 1983. The computing world waited . . . and waited . . . and waited. Finally, after many delays and excuses, the first version of Windows shipped in November 1985, more than a year later than originally promised.

Reviews were mixed, but within a few years, the results were in. The combined power of Microsoft and the leading hardware manufacturers made Windows the standard in the PC world. Apple was not happy. The company sued Microsoft, saying that it stole the "look and feel" of the Macintosh GUI. The result was a long, complicated, and costly legal tangle that wound up hurting both companies. After the dispute was settled, Microsoft invested $150 million in Apple in 1997 to help rescue the troubled company.

Microsoft's Trials

Microsoft has been sued by MITS, Apple, IBM, and the United States government, among others. Here are some of the landmark cases:

1994: Microsoft settles with the U.S. Department of Justice, agreeing to change how it markets Windows.

1997: The Department of Justice sues Microsoft for violating the earlier agreement.

1998: The federal government and twenty states sue Microsoft, accusing it of creating a **monopoly**.

2000: A federal judge rules that Microsoft is a monopoly. The Justice Department asks that the firm be split into two separate companies.

2001: The Justice department drops its demand to break up Microsoft.

MICROSOFT CHANGES

For Microsoft, the 1980s and 1990s were a period of enormous change and growth. Stricken with Hodgkin's disease, Paul Allen left the company, and Steve Ballmer became the company's most important executive after Gates. Today, Ballmer holds the title of Chief Executive Officer (CEO), while Gates is Chairman of the Board and Chief Software Architect. In 1985, Microsoft began moving to its current office campus in Redmond, a Seattle suburb.

The company "went public" in the mid-1980s, selling stock in the firm to raise money for expansion. Since then, despite occasional setbacks, the value of Microsoft

Microsoft's sprawling campus in Redmond, Washington, serves as world headquarters for the huge software firm.

Netscape competed fiercely with Microsoft for control of the Internet browser market. Like most Microsoft rivals, Netscape lost.

stock has skyrocketed. An investment of $10,000 in Microsoft stock in 1987 would be worth millions of dollars today.

During the 1990s, Microsoft released many new software programs and continued to update its Windows operating system. In 1992, Gates was awarded the National Medal of Technology "for his early vision of universal computing at home and in the office; for his technical and business management skills in creating a worldwide technology company; and for his contribution to the development of the personal computer industry." By 1993, Windows had more than twenty-five million licensed users. In 1994, *Forbes* magazine ranked him as the richest man in America, with a personal fortune valued at more than $9 billion.

"BROWSER WARS"

As Microsoft grew, many people feared that the company was becoming too powerful. This was especially true when Microsoft responded to the growth of the Internet by launching its Internet Explorer browser program. Gates feared that if Netscape, a rival firm, was allowed to dominate the Internet with its Netscape Navigator and Communicator software, Microsoft's future business would be hurt.

Microsoft did everything in its power to defeat Netscape. It tied Internet Explorer into the Windows operating system. It pressured PC manufacturers to make Internet Explorer their browser of choice. It gave away Internet Explorer for free—a tactic that made it very difficult for Netscape to make any money from its own browser.

Netscape and other companies complained that Microsoft's behavior was both unfair and illegal. The U.S. Department of Justice took Microsoft to court again and again, and for a while it looked as though Microsoft might be broken up. After years of lawsuits, however, it now appears that Gates's company will continue to survive and thrive.

At a press conference in November 2001, Steve Ballmer and Bill Gates gave their view of a new agreement between Microsoft and the U.S. Department of Justice. The deal penalized Microsoft but did not require the breakup of the company.

CHAPTER 7

GIVING MONEY AWAY

Microsoft was not the only source of change in Bill Gates's life. In a secret ceremony on New Year's Day 1994, he married Melinda French. It was the first marriage for both of them.

Melinda Gates in January 1995, about a year after her marriage to Bill. Their first child, Jennifer Katharine, was born in 1996.

Nine years younger than Gates, Melinda grew up in Dallas, Texas, where her father was an aerospace engineer. She majored in computer science at Duke University; later she earned a degree in business administration, also from Duke. Like Bill, Melinda is intelligent and intense. They met at a company picnic in the late 1980s, soon after she began working for Microsoft as a marketing executive.

When Bill first met Melinda, he was dating another computer software developer, Ann Winblad. She and Gates remain close friends. In 1997, she talked about how Bill might have chosen to marry Melinda. "A relationship with Bill early on is a test," she said. "Are you smart enough? Do you have enough common sense? Can you make the grade? Are you athletic enough? Melinda is Bill's pick. He could have chosen any woman as a wife for life. He has chosen her, and that means she is an exceptional woman."

After Gates became successful with Microsoft in the 1980s, his father urged him to begin giving more money to charity. During the 1990s, Gates set out to become not only the world's richest man but also the world's greatest philanthropist. A philanthropist is someone who helps others, usually by giving large sums of money to worthy causes. Philanthropy—another word for charity—comes from two Greek words that literally mean "love for humanity."

Philanthropy has a long tradition. In the United States and throughout the world, many wealthy people have used their money to help society. Andrew Carnegie, a Scottish-born businessman who made his fortune in U.S. railroads, iron, and steel, was famous for donating millions of dollars to build libraries and museums. Henry Ford, the world-renowned U.S. automobile maker, established a foundation that supports the arts. The Rockefeller family funded Rockefeller Center in New York City among other buildings and museums.

When Bill and Melinda married on New Year's Day 1994, he booked all 250 rooms at a hotel in Hawaii to keep the wedding private. Country star Willie Nelson provided the entertainment. This rather fuzzy photo was taken from a distance.

BILL AND MELINDA GATES FOUNDATION

During the second half of the 1990s, Gates gave away billions of dollars through two foundations. One was the Gates Learning Foundation, which focused on making sure that public libraries had computers and Internet access; the other was the William H. Gates Foundation, which provided money to improve health services for people worldwide.

In January 2000, these two foundations were combined into a new body: the Bill and Melinda Gates Foundation. The new foundation is huge—it has assets of more than $20 billion—but in many ways it tries to be

Andrew Carnegie was a very wealthy businessman who gave generously to worthy causes, just as the Gates Foundation does today.

Located in Seattle on the banks of Lake Washington, the Gates home is worth more than $50 million. It has seven bedrooms, twenty-four bathrooms, six kitchens, six fireplaces, and superbly equipped rooms for meetings, exercise, and entertainment.

How Much Money Has Bill Gates Given Away?

If you had a million dollars, what would you do with it? Would you spend it all on yourself and your friends? Or would you give some of it to people who need help?

Bill Gates has given away billions, and he wants to make sure that it makes a difference. Bill and his wife Melinda are very serious about helping others. Here is how the Bill and Melinda Gates Foundation spent its money in the first two years after it was set up.

World health care	$2.5 billion
Education	$1.5 billion
Libraries	$158 million
Pacific Northwest projects	$262 million
Other projects	$382 million
TOTAL	$4.8 billion

Source: www.gatesfoundation.org/

The Gates Millennium
Scholars Program helps
outstanding students
from low-income minority
families. This photo
shows Bill and Melinda
at center, flanked by four
scholarship winners.

different from other charities. Some old-style philan-
thropies have expensive offices, give money freely, and
hope for results. The offices of the Gates Foundation, in
contrast, are plain and inexpensive. Money is given to
programs that have clear and specific goals, which must
be met.

Overseeing the foundation are Bill Gates's father
and Melinda Gates. Melinda travels to countries such as
India and Haiti to see how money can be applied to help
improve the health of people. William Gates Sr. runs the
foundation's offices in Washington state. The foundation
has a paid staff, but many workers volunteer their time.
Often these volunteers are people who have become rich
through Microsoft, have retired, and now want to give
something back.

Bill and Melinda Gates have set a goal of eliminating
preventable childhood diseases throughout the world.

What Does it Cost to Save a Life?

- A shot of measles vaccine costs a quarter.
- A bed net to prevent the spread of malaria costs four dollars.
- A dose of diarrhea medicine costs thirty-three cents.

The Bill and Melinda Gates Foundation encourages others to donate money to help rid the world of many childhood diseases. Once Bill learned that millions of children around the world die for lack of simple and inexpensive medicines, he decided that "there is no greater issue on earth than the health of our children."

William Gates Sr., his wife Mimi, and former U.S. President Jimmy Carter (left) met Nigerian President Olusegun Obasanjo in March 2002 while touring Africa to focus attention on ways of preventing AIDS.

Bill believes that if children are healthy and well cared for, they can use their energy and intelligence to improve their lives.

Bill Gates thinks hard about how to give his money away. He has said that "spending money intelligently is as difficult as earning it. Giving away money in meaningful ways will be a main preoccupation later in my

At a clinic in India, Bill (right) had a chance to meet with some of the mothers and children who have benefited from Gates Foundation health programs.

life." Gates has also said that he would be glad to sign a document promising to "give away ninety-five percent of my wealth."

"A Wonderful Time to Be Alive"

In his book *The Road Ahead* (1995), Gates takes a very positive view of the world and of the young, smart people who are developing new ways of doing things:

For me, a big part of the fun has always been to hire and work with smart people. I enjoy learning from them. Some of the smart people we're hiring now are a lot younger than I am. I envy them for having grown up with better computers. They're extraordinarily talented and will contribute new visions. . . . I often say I have the best job in the world, and I mean it.

I think this is a wonderful time to be alive. There have never been so many opportunities to do things that were impossible before. It's also the best time ever to start new companies, advance sciences such as medicine that improve quality of life, and stay in touch with friends and relatives.

TIMELINE

1955	William Henry Gates III is born on October 28 in Seattle, Washington
1962	Seattle hosts a World's Fair, which the Gates family attends
1967	Enrolls in Lakeside School, which offers computer access a year later
1973	Enrolls at Harvard University
1975	Founds Microsoft in Albuquerque, New Mexico, with Paul Allen
1976	Drops out of Harvard to work for Microsoft full time
1979	Microsoft moves to the Seattle area
1982	Allen becomes ill and leaves Microsoft the following year
1985	Microsoft releases the first version of its Windows operating system
1986	Microsoft "goes public," selling its stock
1990	Windows 3.0 is released; Microsoft's annual sales exceed $1 billion per year
1994	Marries Melinda French; *Forbes* magazine names him the richest American; Microsoft settles **antitrust** complaint by the U.S. Justice Department
1995	Windows 95 is released
1996	Together with NBC, Microsoft launches MSNBC, a news, talk, and information network
1997	U.S. Justice Department files new antitrust complaint against Microsoft
1998	Windows 98 is released; Microsoft's Internet Explorer takes lead over Netscape in "browser war"
2000	Bill and Melinda Gates Foundation established; judge rules that Microsoft is an illegal monopoly
2001	U.S. Justice Department says it no longer wants to break up Microsoft; Windows XP and the Xbox game system launched

antitrust: laws intended to prevent a powerful company from competing unfairly

BASIC: "Beginners' All-purpose Symbolic Instruction Code," a simple language for telling a computer what to do

bugs: computer software problems

clones: personal computer designs that mimicked the PC built by IBM

cold war: a period of superpower rivalry between the United States and the Soviet Union (mid-1940s to late 1980s)

DOS: short for "disk operating system"

graphical user interface: a way of using a computer that depends on pictures rather than complicated commands

hackers: skilled computer programmers; some hackers use their skills to access data in ways that are immoral or illegal

interface: the way the user and the computer interact

mainframe: a large computer that big businesses use for controlling other computers and for storing information

microcomputer: a personal computer

monopoly: a company with so much power that other companies cannot fairly compete

MS-DOS: the version of DOS developed by Microsoft

nonexclusive licensing agreement: the type of business deal that allows Microsoft to have its software bundled with computers made by many different companies

operating system: the software that tells a computer how to do its most basic tasks

programming: writing in a special language that a computer can understand. BASIC is an example of a programming language

RAM: short for "random-access memory," temporary computer memory that is erased when the computer is turned off

Soviet Union: the former Union of Soviet Socialist Republics, or USSR; the USSR included Russia and other republics that are now independent countries

surreptitiously: secretly

TO FIND OUT MORE

BOOKS

Campbell-Kelly, Martin, and William Aspray. *Computer: A History of the Information Machine*. New York: Basic Books, 1996.

Gates, Bill, with Collins Hemingway. *Business @ the Speed of Thought: Using a Digital Nervous System*. New York: Warner, 1999.

Gates, Bill, with Nathan Myhrvold and Peter Rinearson. *The Road Ahead*. New York: Penguin, 1996.

Gatlin, Jonathan. *Bill Gates: The Path to the Future*. New York: Avon Books, 1999.

Lesinski, Jeanne M. *Bill Gates*. Minneapolis: Lerner, 2000.

Levy, Steven. *Hackers: Heroes of the Computer Revolution*. New York: Penguin, 2001 (rev. ed.).

INTERNET SITES

Bill and Melinda Gates Foundation
www.gatesfoundation.org/
Official site of the foundation, with detailed information about where the money goes.

Bill Gates Net Worth Page
www.quuxuum.org/~evan/bgnw.html
An unofficial site offering various ways to measure just how wealthy Bill Gates is.

Microsoft
www.microsoft.com/
Official site of the Microsoft Corporation.

Paul Allen's Wired World
www.paulallen.com/
Official site of the Microsoft cofounder.

Seattle Times: Microsoft
seattletimes.nwsource.com/html/microsoft
Detailed Microsoft coverage from Gates's hometown newspaper.

INDEX (continued)

About the Author

Lauren Lee is a freelance writer, teacher, and mother of two. She is the author of books for young people and lives in Chicago. She would like to thank the following for their support of this project: Ken Lee, Deirdre and Duncan Lee, New Hope Academy, Harold Bretzlauf, and Mark Sachner.